I0454344

The Millionaire Quick Lane

Unlock the Secrets of Wealth and Enjoy a Lifetime of Prosperity

Charles L. Lake

Table of Content

Introduction

If I were to tell you that there is a way to get wealthy in a few years, rather than waiting for decades, what would you possibly say to that? What if I told you that you could achieve financial independence and live the life of your desires without compromising your health, happiness, or relationships? What would you say to that? Would you believe me if I told you that you could shape your fate rather than going along with the herd?

You may think I'm insane or that I'm attempting to sell you some kind of program that would make you wealthy overnight. You'll likely believe that it's impossible for you to achieve or that it's too wonderful to be true. You may believe that I am lying or that I am delusional.

Well, I'm not it. It is a fact that the majority of people are either unaware of or unwilling to learn. The truth can change your life if you are prepared to listen and act.

The truth is that there is a method to wealth creation that is faster, easier, and more fulfilling than the traditional knowledge of financial planning. A way that is founded on proven ideas, not on luck or hope. A way that is accessible to anybody, regardless of their background, education, or experience. A path that is dubbed the Fast Lane.

The Fast Lane is the road to wealth that allows you to attain financial freedom in a fraction of the time it takes most people. The Fast Lane is the road to prosperity that provides you with control over your income, expenses, and possessions. The fast lane is the road to prosperity that enables you to generate value for others and address their problems or requirements. The Fast Lane is the road to prosperity that helps you leverage, scale, and automate your business and income sources. The Fast Lane is the road to wealth that allows you to enjoy the results of your labor while you are still young and healthy.

The Fast Lane is the road to wealth that I have walked and that many other great entrepreneurs have followed to attain financial freedom and live the life of their desires. The Fastlane is the road to wealth that I want to share with you so that you can achieve the same.

But before I do that, I need to warn you. The fast lane is not for everyone. The Fast Lane is not for the faint of heart, the indolent, or the complacent. The Fastlane is not for the skeptics, the cynics, or the critics. The Fast

Lane is not for the followers, the conformists, or the sheep.

The Fast Lane is for the daring, the ambitious, and the action-takers. The Fast Lane is for the believers, the optimists, and the dreamers. The Fast Lane is for the leaders, the innovators, and the rebels.

The Fast Lane is for you if you are ready to disrupt the status quo, violate the rules, and build your reality.

The Fastlane is for you if you are ready to unlock the secrets of wealth and experience a lifetime of prosperity.

Are you ready?

If you are, then buckle up and get ready for the trip of your life. In this book, I'm going to show you how to enter the fast lane, accelerate your wealth-building, and reach your destination of financial freedom.

But before we hit the road, let me tell you a little bit about me and how I discovered Fastlane. Let me tell you why I wrote this book and what you may expect from it. Let me tell you why the fast lane is the finest path to prosperity and how it differs from the slow lane, which is the road that most people take.

The Slow Lane is the road to wealth that is focused on saving, investing, and working hard for decades. The Slow Lane is the path to prosperity that is taught by the mainstream media, the education system, and the culture. The Slow Lane is the route to prosperity that is pursued by the majority of people who are locked in the rat race, living paycheck to paycheck, and dreaming of a better future. The Slow Lane is the road to wealth that is slow, dangerous, and frustrating. The Slow Lane is the route to prosperity that is based on circumstances that are outside of your control, such as the economy, the stock market, inflation, taxes, and the government. The Slow Lane is the path to prosperity restricted by your time, money, and expenses. The Slow Lane is the road to wealth that is built on consumption, not creation. The slow lane is the route to wealth that is focused on sacrificing your life for money instead of making your money work for you. The Slow Lane is the path to wealth that I used to follow and that many people still follow, to their peril. The Slow Lane is the path to prosperity that I wish to disclose so that you can avoid it.

But don't take my word for it. Let me show you some data and instances that will highlight the difference between the fast lane and the slow lane and why the fast lane is the superior road to prosperity.

According to the U.S. Census Bureau, the median household income in the United States in 2020 was $68,703. That means that half of the households earned more than that, and half earned less. That also means that the average household income was roughly $70,000, which is not significantly higher than the   median.
Now, let's imagine that you are an ordinary American, making $70,000 each year. Let's also assume that you are following the Slow Lane recommendation of saving 10% of your income, investing it in a diverse portfolio of stocks and bonds, and expecting a 10% yearly return, which is the historical average of the S&P 500 index.

How long do you think it will take you to

become a billionaire if you follow this plan? The answer is 31 years.

That's right. It will take you 31 years to collect $1 million if you save and invest $7,000 every year a 10% annual return. And that's assuming that you never increase your expenditure, never pay taxes, never confront inflation, never lose money in the market, and never have any crises or unforeseen expenses.

That's also presuming that $1 million is enough for you to retire and live well for the rest of your life, which is highly unlikely, given the rising cost of living and the falling value of money.

In other words, the Slow Lane plan is a strategy to become a millionaire when you are elderly, assuming you are lucky.

But what if you are not lucky? What if you experience a recession, a market crash, a job loss, a divorce, a health crisis, or any other setback that can derail your plan? What if you want to have a better lifestyle, travel the world, pursue your passions, or support your family and friends? What if you want to have more freedom, more options, and more impact? Then the slow lane plan is not for you. The Slow Lane plan is a plan to be poor, miserable, and dependent.

But there is a better way. A strategy that can make you a billionaire in a few years, instead of decades. A way that can make you rich, happy, and independent.

That way is the Fast Lane. The Fastlane is the road to wealth that is focused on generating, not consuming. The

Fastlane is the road to wealth that is built on having your money work for you, instead of selling your life for money. The Fastlane is the road to prosperity that is built on elements that are within your control, such as your value, your business, and your income streams. The Fastlane is the road to prosperity that is not restricted by your time, your income, or your expenses. The Fast Lane is the road to wealth that is fast, safe, and fulfilling.

The Fastlane is the road to wealth that I have walked, and that many other great entrepreneurs have followed, to attain financial freedom and live the life of our desires. The Fast Lane is the road to wealth that I want to share with you so that you can achieve the same. But how does the Fast Lane work? How can you enter the Fast Lane, accelerate your wealth building, and reach your destination of financial freedom?

That's what this book is all about. In this book, I will expose the secrets of Fast Lane and show you how to use them in your own life. I will teach you the principles, techniques, and tactics that will enable you to create value for others and produce large income streams. I will show you how to leverage, scale, and automate your business and income streams and build your wealth tenfold. I will show you how to enjoy the results of your labor while you are still young and healthy.

In this book, I will show you how to become a millionaire in Fast Lane.

Are you ready to join me?

If you are, then let's get started.

The Millionaire Quick Lane

The Millionaire Quick Lane

Chapter 1
The Law of Acceleration.

What is the difference between a snail and a cheetah?

The answer is obvious: **Speed.**

A snail moves at a pace of 0.03 miles per hour, while a cheetah can gallop up to 75 miles per hour. That means that a cheetah can travel the same distance that a snail takes an hour in less than a minute.

Now, what is the difference between a slow lanner and a fast lanner?

The answer is likewise obvious: **Speed.** A slow lanner moves at a pace of 10% each year, while a fast lanner can grow at a rate of 100% per month. That means that a fast lanner can obtain the same riches that a slow lanner takes a decade to obtain in less than a year.

How is that possible?

The answer is simple: **Acceleration.** Acceleration is the rate of change of speed. Acceleration is the key to wealth generation. Acceleration is the secret of Fastlane. But how can you accelerate your wealth creation? How do you boost your speed and reach your target faster than anyone else? The answer is threefold:

leverage, systems, and scalability.

Leverage, systems, and scale are the three elements that may accelerate your wealth generation and make you rich faster than anyone else. Leverage, systems, and scale are the three elements that successful entrepreneurs employ to build their firms and produce large cash streams. Leverage, systems, and scale are the three elements that you need to grasp if you want to enter the fast lane and attain financial freedom. Let me explain each of these ideas in depth, and show you how to use them in your own life.

Leverage

Leverage is the power to magnify your efforts, resources, and results. Leverage is the power to enhance your effect, influence, and income. Leverage is the basic principle of acceleration because it allows you to increase your speed without increasing your work. Leverage is the basic principle of acceleration because it allows you to achieve more with the same or less input. Leverage is the first concept of acceleration because it allows you to produce value faster, easier, and cheaper than others.

There are several sorts of leverage that you can utilize to accelerate your wealth growth, such as:

• **Financial Leverage:** Leveraging other people's money (OPM) to support your business or investments, and achieve a higher return than the cost of capital.

• **Human Leverage:** Leveraging other people's time (OPT) to execute jobs or duties that you don't want to do, can't do, or shouldn't do, and focusing on your core competencies and highest-value activities.

• **Technological Leverage:** Leveraging other people's tools (OPT) to automate, simplify, or enhance your processes, goods, or services, and raise your efficiency, quality, or performance.

- **Intellectual Leverage:** Leveraging other people's knowledge (OPK) to learn, enhance, or create your skills, ideas, or solutions, and boost your expertise, creativity, or differentiation.

- **Network Leverage:** Using other people's contacts (OPC) to access, connect, or interact with new customers, partners, or mentors, and boosting your exposure, credibility, or opportunities.

The more leverage you apply, the faster you can accelerate your wealth growth.

The more leverage you employ, the more value you may produce for others and yourself.

The more leverage you apply, the more money you can produce from your business or investments.

But how can you use leverage effectively?

How can you avoid the traps and hazards of leverage?

How do you determine the best balance of leverage?

The key is to use leverage intelligently, responsibly, and strategically.

The answer is to use leverage as a means, not as an aim.

The key is to utilize leverage to serve your cause, not to enslave you.

Here are some ideas on how to apply leverage properly:

• Use leverage only when you have a clear goal, a solid plan, and a proven system for your business or investments. Don't use leverage to gamble, speculate, or chase flashy items.

• Use leverage only when you have a good

cash flow, a high-profit margin, and a robust balance sheet for your firm or investments. Don't use leverage to pay your losses, expenses, or debts.

• Use leverage only when you have a competitive advantage, a distinctive value offer, and a loyal client base for your business or investments. Don't use leverage to compete on price, features, or quantity.

• Use leverage only when you have a high degree of control, a low level of risk, and a high level of profit for your business or assets. Don't utilize leverage to expose oneself to external circumstances, uncertainties, or obligations.

• Use leverage only when you have a favorable impact, a positive influence, and a positive income for your business or investments.

Don't use leverage to injure, exploit, or cheat people. Leverage is a strong weapon that can accelerate your wealth generation and make you rich faster than anybody else. But leverage is also a double-edged blade that may cut both ways. Leverage may make you or break you, depending on how you utilize it.

Use leverage properly, ethically, and strategically, and you will enter the fast lane and attain financial freedom.

Systems

Systems are the set of rules, processes, and structures that control your business or assets. Systems are the set of inputs, outputs, and feedback loops that determine your results. Systems are the set of components, operations, and interactions that create your value.

Systems are the second principle of acceleration because they allow you to raise your speed without increasing your work. Systems are the second principle of acceleration because they allow you to achieve more with the same or less input. Systems are the second principle of acceleration since they allow you to create value consistently, reliably, and predictably.

There are several benefits to having systems for your business or investments, such as:

• Systems save you time, energy, and money by automating, simplifying, or eliminating your chores, functions, or expenses.

• Systems boost your efficiency, quality, and performance by standardizing, optimizing, or upgrading your processes, goods, or services.

• Systems boost your scalability, sustainability, and profitability by reproducing, increasing, or diversifying your outputs, markets, or income sources.

• Systems boost your flexibility, adaptability, and invention by testing, measuring, or enhancing your inputs, outputs, or feedback loops.

• Systems promote your independence, security, and happiness by decreasing, delegating, or outsourcing your involvement, dependence, or stress.

The more systems you have, the faster you can accelerate your money production. The more systems you have, the more value you can produce for others and yourself. The more systems you have, the more income you can create from your business or assets. But how can you develop systems effectively? How can you develop, implement, and manage systems? How can you improve, upgrade, or replace systems?

The answer is to follow a methodical approach, a proven technique, and a best practice. The answer is to follow the system of systems.

Here are some instructions on how to construct systems properly:

• Define your mission, vision, and goals for your business or investments. What are you aiming to achieve? Why are you doing it? How will you quantify it?

• Identify your value proposition, target market, and client needs for your business or investments. What are you offering? Who are you serving? What are their problems or desires?

• Analyze your strengths, weaknesses, opportunities, and threats for your business or investments. What are you good at? What are you awful at? What are the external influences that can assist or hurt you?

• Design your procedures, goods, and services for your business or investments. What are the features, benefits, and costs that you provide?

• Implement your procedures, test your results, and collect feedback for your business or investments. How will you execute, measure, and improve your value creation? What are the measurements, indicators, and benchmarks that you use? What are the sources, methods, and channels that you get feedback from?

• Manage your systems, assess your performance, and make improvements for your business or investments. How will you sustain, optimize, and enhance your value creation? What are the standards, rules, and processes that you follow? What are the adjustments, upgrades, or innovations that you make? Systems are a strong instrument that can accelerate your wealth development and make you rich faster than anyone else. But systems are also dynamic entities that can evolve, adapt, or become obsolete. Systems can work for you or against you, depending on how you construct them.

Create systems effectively, efficiently, and

excellently, and you will reach Fastlane and gain financial freedom.

Scale

Scale is growing your production, effect, and income without increasing your input, effort, or expense. Scale is the ability to service more clients, solve more problems, and create more income. Scale is the ability to grow your business or assets beyond their current size and reach new levels of profitability and influence.

Scale is the third principle of acceleration because it allows you to raise your speed without increasing your work. Scale is the third principle of acceleration because it allows you to achieve more with the same or less input. Scale is the third principle of acceleration since it allows you to produce value exponentially, massively, and endlessly.

Several elements affect your ability to expand your business or assets, such as:

• **Demand:** The level of interest, desire, or need that your customers have for your products or services. The larger the demand, the easier it is to scale your business or investments. The smaller the demand, the tougher it is to scale your business or investments. To grow your demand, you need to produce value that is relevant, useful, and attractive to your target market. You need to solve an issue, meet a need, or satisfy a desire that your consumers have. You need to offer a solution that is better, faster, or cheaper than your competition. You need to explain your value offer clearly, eloquently, and consistently to your potential customers.

• **Supply:** The level of availability,

accessibility, or cost of your items or services. The higher the supply, the easier it is to scale your business or investments. The lower the supply, the tougher it is to scale your business or investments. To grow your supply, you need to produce value that is scalable, replicable, and sustainable for your business or investments. You need to develop, deliver, and capture value efficiently, effectively, and beautifully. You need to optimize your processes, products, and services to lower your expenses, raise your quality, and improve your performance. You need to use your resources, tools, and partners to enhance your capability, reach, and effect.

• **Distribution:** The level of exposure, awareness, or attraction of your items or services. The higher the distribution, the easier it is to scale your business or assets. The lower the distribution, the tougher it is to scale your firm or investments. To enhance your distribution, you need to provide value that is visible, attractive, and viral for your target market. You need to promote, market, and sell your items or services effectively, efficiently, and excellently. You need to choose the correct channels, platforms, and techniques to reach your target clients. You need to build a unique brand, an engaging message, and a committed community.

The more you can balance these aspects, the faster you can scale your business or investments. The more you can balance these aspects, the more value you can produce for others and yourself. The more you can balance these aspects, the more money you can create from your business or assets. But how can you balance these things effectively?

How do you discover the appropriate point of scale for your business or investments? How can you avoid the pitfalls and hazards of scale?

The answer is to employ scale properly, responsibly, and strategically. The answer is to use scale as a means, not as an aim. The answer is to leverage size to serve your objective, not to enslave you.

Here are some pointers on how to utilize scale properly:

• Use scale only when you have a proven product-market fit, favorable consumer feedback, and a significant product demand for your business or investments. Don't use scale to push, influence, or fool your customers into buying your products or services.

• Use scale only when you have a stable supply chain, a robust delivery system, and constant product quality for your business or investments. Don't use scale to compromise, surrender, or neglect your product's standards, ethics, or principles.

• Use scale only when you have a defined distribution strategy, a cost-effective marketing plan, and a strong conversion rate for your business or investments. Don't use scale to spam, harass, or alienate your potential consumers or partners.

• Use scale only when you have a solid cash flow, a high-profit margin, and a robust balance sheet for your firm or investments. Don't utilize scale to cover your losses, expenses, or debts.

• Use scale only when you have a positive impact, a positive influence, and a favorable income for your business or investments. Don't utilize scale to injure, exploit, or cheat people.

Scale is a strong instrument that can accelerate your wealth development and make you rich faster than anybody else. But scale is also a complex problem that can overwhelm, worry, or ruin you. Scale can work for you or against you, depending on how you use it.

Use scale properly, ethically, and strategically, and you will enter Fastlane and attain financial freedom.

The Millionaire Quick Lane

Chapter 2

The Psychology of Wealth

Money is the byproduct, not the source, of riches. Money is the byproduct, not the source, of success. Money is the consequence, not the origin, of value.

Mindset is the set of ideas, attitudes, and habits that form your thoughts, feelings, and behaviors. Mindset is the set of beliefs, expectations, and aspirations that drive your actions, behaviors, and results. Mindset is the set of beliefs, values, and standards that guide your life, career, and relationships. Mindset is the difference between a rich person and a poor person. Mindset is the difference between a fast learner and a slow learner.

Mindset is the second principle of wealth development because it defines your pace, direction, and goal. Mindset is the second principle of wealth creation because it defines your potential, performance, and advancement. Mindset is the second fundamental of wealth building because it defines your value, effect, and income. Two types of attitudes affect your wealth creation: the fixed mindset and the growing mindset.

The fixed mindset is the assumption that your abilities, talents, and intelligence are fixed and cannot be changed. The fixed mindset is the assumption that your success or failure is decided by your genes, environment, or luck. The fixed mindset is the assumption that your value, effect, and money are limited and scarce.

The fixed attitude is the mindset of the impoverished, the slow lane, and the loser.

The locked mindset is the thinking that holds you back from pursuing your aspirations, attaining your goals, and creating your wealth. The fixed attitude is the thinking that makes you fearful, doubtful, and complacent.

The growth mindset is the concept that your abilities, talents, and intelligence can be increased and enhanced. The growth mentality is the concept that your success or failure is influenced by your activities, decisions, and efforts. The growth mindset is the belief that your value, impact, and income are infinite and abundant. The growth mindset is the mindset of the rich, the fastener, and the winner. The growth mentality is the mindset that helps you pursue your aspirations, achieve your goals, and create wealth. The growth mindset is the mindset that makes you confident, optimistic, and proactive.

The more you adopt a growth mindset, the faster you can accelerate your wealth production. The more you adopt a development mindset, the more value you can produce for others and yourself. The more you adopt a growth mindset, the more revenue you can earn from your business or assets. But how can you embrace the growth mindset effectively?

How can you transcend the fixed mindset that limits your potential, performance, and progress?

How can you build a good mindset, a strong work ethic, and a passion for what you do?

The answer is to follow a psychological approach, a validated methodology, and a best practice. The key is to follow the psychology of prosperity.

Here are some steps on how to adopt the development mindset properly:

• Identify your limiting beliefs, worries, doubts, and excuses that hold you back from pursuing your ambitions, attaining your objectives, and building your wealth. What are the negative ideas, feelings, and actions that keep you from entering Fastlane and obtaining financial freedom?

• Challenge your limiting beliefs, fears, doubts, and excuses using evidence, logic, and reason. What are the facts, evidence, and instances that contradict your negative beliefs, attitudes, and actions? What are the alternate explanations, views, and possibilities that support your positive ideas, feelings, and actions?

• Replace your limiting beliefs, worries,

doubts, and excuses with powerful beliefs, courage, confidence, and action. What are the positive ideas, attitudes, and behaviors that enable you to enter Fastlane and attain financial freedom? What are the affirmations, visions, and goals that encourage you to pursue your aspirations, achieve your goals, and generate your wealth?

• Practice your empowering beliefs, courage, confidence, and action daily, weekly, and monthly. What are the habits, routines, and rituals that reinforce your good thoughts, feelings, and actions? What are the abilities, knowledge, and methods that boost your potential, performance, and progress? What is the feedback, awards, and acknowledgments that recognize your achievements, successes, and results?

The more you follow these principles, the

more you can embrace the development mentality. The more you follow these methods, the more you can transcend fixed thinking. The more you follow these principles, the more you can create a positive attitude, a strong work ethic, and a passion for what you do.

The psychology of money is a strong weapon that can accelerate your wealth generation and make you rich faster than anyone else. But the psychology of wealth is also a personal journey that involves commitment, discipline, and endurance. The psychology of wealth can work for you or against you, depending on how you use it.

Use the psychology of wealth effectively, efficiently, and excellently, and you will enter Fast Lane and gain financial freedom.

The Millionaire Quick Lane

The Millionaire Quick Lane

Chapter 3:

The Art of Value Creation

What is the difference between a creator and a consumer? The answer is **Value.**

Value is the advantage, utility, or satisfaction that your items or services bring to your customers. Value is the difference, improvement, or transformation that your products or services create in your customers' lives. Value is the reason, objective, or purpose for which your customers acquire your items or services. Value is the distinction between a producer and a consumer. Value is the difference between a fast lanner and a slow lanner. Value is the difference between a producer and   a   parasite. Value is the third principle of wealth building because it affects your pace, direction, and destination. Value is the third principle of wealth creation because it defines your potential, performance, and advancement. Value is the third principle of wealth development because it defines your income, effect, and influence.

There are two forms of value that you may create for your customers:

The inherent value and the perceived value.

Inherent value is the objective, measurable, and tangible worth that your products or services bring to your customers. The inherent value is the value that is founded on facts, data, and proof. The inherent value is the value that is based on characteristics, advantages, and expenses. Perceived value is the subjective, emotional, and intangible value that your products or services bring to your customers. The perceived value is the value that is dependent on thoughts, sentiments, and impressions. The perceived value is the value that is based on stories, symbols, and meanings.

The more value you create, the faster you can accelerate your wealth growth. The more value you create, the more clients you can attract, retain, and satisfy. The more value you create, the more income you can generate from your business or investments.

But how can you produce value effectively? How can you find opportunities where you can create value for others and answer their challenges or needs? How can you investigate your target market, evaluate your ideas, build your solutions, and launch your offerings?

The answer is to follow a creative approach, a proven technique, and a best practice. The answer is to follow the art of value creation.

Here are some steps on how to build value properly:

• Identify your passion, abilities, and expertise for your business or investments. What are you good at? What do you enjoy doing? What do you know a lot about?

• Identify your challenges, needs, or desires for your business or investments. What are the challenges, hurts, or frustrations that you encounter or have faced? What are the solutions, wins, or pleasures that you want or have wanted?

• Identify your market, specialization, and audience for your business or investments. Who are the folks who share your concerns, wants, or desires? Who are the people who can benefit from your passion, talents, or expertise?

• Research your market, niche, and audience for your business or investments. What are the trends, opportunities, and risks that affect your market, niche, or audience? What are the existing products or services that serve your market, niche, or audience? What are the gaps, defects, or limitations of the existing products or services?

• Generate ideas for your products or services for your business or investments. How can you create value for your market, specialty, or audience? How can you address their issues, serve their wants, or satisfy their desires? How can you differentiate yourself from your competitors?

• Validate your ideas for your products or services for your business or investments. How can you test your assumptions, hypotheses, and forecasts regarding your ideas? How can you gather feedback, statistics, and proof to support or reject your ideas? How can you quantify your value proposition, client happiness, and market potential?

• Design your items or services for your business or investments. How can you bring your thoughts into reality? How can you construct a prototype, a minimally viable product, or a beta version of your products or services? How can you optimize your features, benefits, and expenses to maximize your value creation?

• Launch your items or services for your business or investments. How can you introduce your products or services to your market, niche, or audience? How can you establish a launch strategy, a marketing plan, and a sales funnel for your products or services? How do you generate buzz, traction, and money for your products or services? The more you follow these principles, the more you may create value for others and yourself. The more you follow these procedures, the more you can uncover chances where you can generate value and solve problems or needs. The more you follow these procedures, the more you can research your target market, validate your ideas, build your solutions, and launch your offers.

The art of value creation is a strong instrument that can accelerate your wealth development and make you rich faster than anybody else. But the art of value creation is also a personal journey that requires curiosity, inspiration, and experimentation. The skill of value creation can work for you or against you, depending on how you employ it.

Use the art of value creation effectively, efficiently, and excellently, and you will enter Fast Lane and gain financial freedom.

Chapter 4
The Power of Marketing

What is the difference between a product and a brand?

The answer is **Marketing.**

Marketing is the process of communicating, delivering, and exchanging your value proposition with your clients. Marketing is the process of building, maintaining, and enhancing your relationship with your customers. Marketing is the process of influencing, persuading, and encouraging your clients to buy your products or services. Marketing is the difference between a product and a brand. Marketing is the difference between a fast learner and a slow learner.

Marketing is the difference between a seller and a leader.

Marketing is the fourth pillar of wealth development because it defines your speed, direction, and destination. Marketing is the fourth pillar of wealth building because it defines your potential, performance, and advancement. Marketing is the fourth pillar of wealth development because it determines your revenue, effect, and influence. There are two sorts of marketing that you can employ to create demand for your products or services: outward marketing and inbound marketing.

Outbound marketing is the form of marketing that promotes your value proposition to your customers. Outbound marketing is the form of marketing that interrupts, distracts, or disturbs your customers. Outbound marketing is a form of marketing that is centered on advertising, promotion, or sales.

Inbound marketing is the form of marketing that brings your customers to your value proposition. Inbound marketing is the form of marketing that educates, entertains, or engages your customers. Inbound marketing is a form of marketing that is built on content, community, or recommendations.

The more effective your marketing is, the faster you can accelerate your revenue generation. The more effective your marketing is, the more clients you can attract, retain, and satisfy. The more effective your marketing is, the more cash you can create from your business or assets. But how can you do marketing effectively? How do you attract clients who are willing to pay for your value offer and develop demand for your products or services? How do you build a unique selling proposition (USP), craft a captivating message, identify the correct channels, and measure your results? The answer is to follow a strategic strategy, an established methodology, and a best practice. The answer is to follow the power of marketing.

Here are some steps on how to do marketing properly:

• Define your USP for your products or services. What makes your products or services distinct, better, or unique from your competitors? What is the key benefit, advantage, or solution that your products or services bring to your customers? What is the core message, promise, or value that your products or services communicate to your customers?

• Craft your message for your items or services. How can you explain your USP to your clients in a clear, succinct, and catchy way? How can you appeal to your customers' emotions, wants, or desires? How can you persuade your customers to take action, such as buying, subscribing, or sharing your products or services?

• Choose your channels for your items or services. How can you reach your customers where they are, when they are, and how they are? How can you identify the most relevant, effective, and efficient channels for your products or services, such as online, offline, or hybrid? How can you maximize your channels for your products or services, such as SEO, social media, email, or events?

• Measure your results for your products or

services. How can you track, analyze, and assess your marketing performance and outcomes? How can you apply the correct metrics, tools, and methodologies to measure your marketing results, such as traffic, leads, conversions, or revenue? How can you use the feedback, data, and insights to better your marketing plans, methods, and actions? The more you follow these guidelines, the more you can accomplish marketing effectively. The more you follow these processes, the more you may attract clients who are willing to pay for your value proposition and develop demand for your products or services. The more you follow these processes, the more you can establish a distinctive selling proposition, craft a captivating message, choose the correct channels, and measure your outcomes. The power of marketing is a powerful tool that can accelerate your wealth development and make you rich faster than anybody else. But the power of marketing is also a complex problem that takes imagination, expertise, and experience. The power of marketing can work for you or against you, depending on how you employ it.

the marketing power of marketing effectively, efficiently, and excellently, and you will enter Fastlane and gain financial freedom.

Chapter 5
The Secrets of Scaling

What is the difference between a small firm and a huge business?

The solution is **Scale.**

Scale is growing your production, effect, and income without increasing your input, effort, or expense. Scale is the ability to service more clients, solve more problems, and create more income. Scale is the ability to grow your firm beyond its current size and reach new levels of profitability and influence.

Scale is the difference between a small business and a big one. Scale is the difference between a fast lanner and a slow lanner. Scale is the difference between a leader and a follower. Scale is the fifth principle of wealth development because it defines your pace, direction, and destination. Scale is the fifth principle of wealth creation because it defines your potential, performance, and advancement.

Scale is the sixth principle of wealth development because it defines your income, effect, and influence.

There are several ways to scale your business, such as:

• **Delegate tasks:** Appoint, train, and monitor your employees or contractors to accomplish jobs or functions that you don't want to do, can't do, or shouldn't do, and focus on your core talents and highest-value activities.

• **Outsource functions:** Employ, manage,

and work with external providers or agencies to undertake functions or processes that are not your core competencies or competitive advantages and decrease your costs, risks, or liabilities.

• **Automate processes:** Employ, integrate, and optimize software, hardware, or systems to automate, simplify, or enhance your processes, goods, or services, and raise your efficiency, quality, or performance.

• **Leverage partnerships:** Partner, network, or cooperate with other firms, organizations, or influencers that have complementary talents, resources, or audiences and boost your exposure, credibility, or opportunities.

• **Expand markets:** Enter, explore, or dominate new or current markets, segments, or niches that have high demand, low supply, or high profitability for your products or services, and grow your customer base, market share, or revenue streams.

• **Diversify products or services:** Produce, launch, or acquire new or existing products or services that are linked, complementary, or supplemental to your core products or services and boost your value proposition, customer happiness, or income streams.

The more you scale your firm, the faster you can accelerate your wealth development. The more you scale your business, the more value you can produce for others and yourself. The more you grow your firm, the more money you can create from your business or investments. But how do you scale your firm effectively? How can you determine the best approach to scaling your business? How can you avoid the problems and risks of scaling your business? The key is to scale your firm sensibly, ethically, and strategically. The answer is to scale your business as a means, not as an end. The answer is to scale your business to serve your mission, not to enslave you.

Here are some pointers on how to scale your business properly:

• Scale your business only when you have a proven product-market fit, favorable customer feedback, and a significant product demand for your business. Don't scale your business to coerce, manipulate, or fool your clients into buying your products or services.

• Scale your business only when you have a stable supply chain, a robust delivery system, and consistent product quality for your firm. Don't scale your business to compromise, sacrifice, or neglect your product standards, ethics, or principles.

• Scale your business only when you have a clear distribution strategy, a cost-effective marketing plan, and a good conversion rate for your business. Don't scale your business to spam, annoy, or alienate your potential consumers or partners.

• Scale your firm only when you have good cash flow, a healthy profit margin, and a robust balance sheet for your business. Don't scale your business to cover your losses, expenses, or obligations.

• Scale your business only when you have a positive impact, a positive influence, and a favorable income for your firm. Don't scale your business to injure, exploit, or cheat others.

Scale is a strong instrument that can accelerate your wealth development and make you rich faster than anybody else. But size is also a challenging problem that takes vision, expertise, and experience. Scale can work for you or against you, depending on how you use it.

Scale your firm sensibly, responsibly, and strategically, and you will reach Fastlane and achieve financial freedom.

Conclusion

Congratulations! You have mastered the secrets of Fastlane, the route to wealth that allows you to reach financial freedom in a fraction of the time it takes other people. You have studied the five concepts of wealth creation that can accelerate your wealth generation and make you rich faster than anybody else:

• **Leverage:** The ability to do more with less, double your efforts, resources, and outcomes, and amplify your impact, influence, and income.

• **Systems:** The set of rules, methods, and structures that regulate your business or investments, determine your results, and produce your value.

• **Value:** The benefit, utility, or satisfaction that your products or services bring to your consumers; the difference, improvement, or transformation that your products or services create in your customers' lives; and the reason, motive, or purpose that your customers acquire your products or services.

• **Marketing:** The process of communicating, providing, and exchanging your value proposition to your customers; developing, maintaining, and enhancing your relationship with them; and influencing, persuading, and inspiring them to acquire your products or services.

• **Scale:** The ability to expand your output, impact, and income without increasing your input, effort, or expense; service more customers; solve more problems; produce more revenue; and develop your firm beyond its current scale and achieve new levels of profitability and impact.

You have also learned how to implement these ideas in your own life by following the procedures, advice, and examples that I have provided in each chapter. You have learned how to identify, challenge, and replace your limiting beliefs, fears, doubts, and excuses that hold you back from pursuing your dreams, achieving your objectives, and building your wealth. You have learned how to establish a positive attitude, a strong work ethic, and a passion for what you do.

You have learned how to enter the fast lane, accelerate your wealth generation, and reach your objective of financial freedom. But learning is not enough. Knowledge is pointless without action. Action is the bridge between your dreams and your realities.

Action is the key to wealth building. Action is the secret of Fastlane.

That's why I want to push you to take action today and start building your money through Fastlane. I want to push you to use what you have learned in this book in your own life. I want to challenge you to create value for others and yourself and build large income streams.

To help you with that, I have prepared some action steps or exercises that you can perform right now, or as soon as possible, to get started on your Fast Lane adventure.

Here they are:

• **Action Step 1:** Write down your vision, goals, and action plan for your wealth creation. What do you wish to achieve? Why do you want to achieve it? How will you achieve it? Be specific, practical, and measurable. Break down your enormous goals into smaller, realistic, and doable actions. Set a deadline for each phase and track your progress.

• **Action Step 2:** Identify your passion, skills, and expertise that you can utilize to produce value for others and yourself. What are you good at? What do you enjoy doing? What do you know a lot about? Make a list of your abilities, talents, and hobbies. Choose one or a few that you can convert into a business or an investment.

• **Action Step 3:** Identify your challenges, wants, or desires that you can address or satisfy using your passion, talents, or experience. What are the challenges, hurts, or frustrations that you encounter or have faced? What are the solutions, wins, or pleasures that you want or have wanted? Make a list of your concerns, needs, or desires. Choose one or a few that you can turn into a product or a service.

• **Action Step 4:** Identify your market, specialty, and audience that share your challenges, requirements, or ambitions and can profit from your passion, talents, or knowledge. Those are the folks that have the same or comparable problems, wants, or desires as you? Who are the folks who can afford, appreciate, and pay for your products or services? Make a list of your possible clients, sectors, or niches. Choose one or a few that you can target and serve.

• **Action Step 5:** Research your market, niche, and audience to find out their trends, opportunities, and threats, their existing products or services, and any gaps, defects, or shortcomings. What are the external elements that affect your market, niche, or audience? What are the items or services that they are now utilizing or buying? What are the difficulties, wants, or desires that they still have or are not pleased with? Use online or offline sources, such as Google, Amazon, social media, forums, blogs, magazines, books, surveys, interviews, etc., to obtain information, data, and insights. Analyze and combine your data to determine your competitive edge, unique value proposition, and market potential.

• **Action Step 6**: Generate ideas for your products or services that can provide value for your market, niche, and audience, solve their issues, fulfill their wants, or satisfy their desires, and separate yourself from your competition. How can you develop, provide, and collect value for your customers? How can you solve their issues, fulfill their wants, or satisfy their desires better, faster, or cheaper than your competitors? How do you make your products or services unique, memorable, and remarkable?

Use brainstorming, mind mapping, or other creative strategies to produce as many ideas as possible. Choose one or a few that you can turn into a prototype, a minimally viable product, or a beta version.

How can you gather input from your potential clients, partners, or mentors? How can you quantify your value generation, customer happiness, and market potential? Use online or offline tools, such as landing pages, websites, social media, email, surveys, interviews, focus groups, etc., to validate your ideas. Use metrics, indicators, and benchmarks, such as traffic, leads, conversions, revenue, etc., to measure your results. Use feedback, data, and insights to support or reject your ideas, and make adjustments, changes, or pivots as needed.

• **Action Step 8:** Design your products or services by converting your ideas into reality, building a prototype, a minimal viable product, or a beta version, and optimizing your features, benefits, and costs to maximize your value generation. How can you bring your thoughts into reality? How can you construct a prototype, a minimally viable product, or a beta version of your products or services? How can you optimize your features, benefits, and expenses to maximize your value creation? Use online or offline tools, such as software, hardware, systems, and tools, to design your products or services. Use the lean startup, agile, or scrum approaches to build, measure, and learn from your goods or services. Use the comments, data, and insights from your validation to improve your products or services.

• **Action Step 9:** Launch your products or services by exposing them to your market, niche, and audience, building a launch strategy, a marketing plan, and a sales funnel, and generating buzz, traction, and money for your products or services. How can you introduce your products or services to your market, specialty, and audience? How can you establish a launch strategy, a marketing plan, and a sales funnel for your products or services? How do you generate buzz, traction, and money for your products or services? Use online or offline channels, platforms, and techniques, such as websites, social media, email, events, etc., to introduce your products or services. Use the power of marketing, as discussed in Chapter 4, to express, deliver, and convey your value proposition to your customers and influence, persuade, and motivate them to buy your products or services.

These are the action steps or exercises that you can take right now, or as soon as feasible, to get started on your Fast Lane trip. These are the action steps or exercises that will help you apply what you have learned in this book in your own life. These are the actions or exercises that will help you create value for others and yourself and produce large income streams.

But don't stop here. Don't let this book be another book that you read and forget. Don't let this book be another book that you put on your shelf and never use. Don't let this book be another book that you waste your time, money, or energy on.

Let this book be the book that changes your life. Let this book be the book that motivates you to take action. Let this book be the book that helps you enter the Fastlane and attain financial freedom.

The fast lane is waiting for you. The fast lane is calling you. The Fastlane is inviting you. Are you ready to enter the fast lane? If you are, then don't hesitate. Don't procrastinate. Don't delay.

Take action immediately and start building your wealth with Fast Lane.

You have the power and the potential to shape your future.

You have the secrets and the tactics to unleash the money and the freedom that you deserve.

You have the fast lane.

Now, go and make it happen.

I wish you all the best on your Fast Lane trip. I hope this book has been helpful, valuable, and enjoyable for you. I hope this book has been the catalyst, the guide, and the mentor for your Fast Lane trip. I hope this book has been the start, the spark, and the fuel for your Fastlane   trip.
Thank you for reading this book. Thank you for joining Fastlane. Thank you for being a Fast lanner.

Now, go and make it happen.

You can do it.

You are a fast lanner and a millionaire in the making.

You are a wealth creator.

You are a value creator.

You are a maker.

You are great.

You are the Fast Lane.

This is the end

www.ingramcontent.com/pod-product-compliance
Lightning Source LLC
Chambersburg PA
CBHW062236290526
45794CB00006B/2309

* 9 7 9 8 8 7 3 3 9 9 5 6 7 *